THINKING ABOUT VENEZUELA
WITH ENERGY

An Invitation to Work Together

Blas Antonio Herrera Pérez

All rights reserved. The total or partial reproduction of this work is not allowed, nor its incorporation into a computer system, or its transmission in any form or by any means (electronic, mechanical, photocopying, recording, or otherwise) without the prior written permission of the copyright holder is a violation of these rights and may constitute a crime against intellectual property

The content of this work is the responsibility of the author and does not necessarily reflect the views of the publishing house. All texts and images were provided by the author, who is solely responsible for their rights.

Published by Ibukku, LLC
www.ibukku.com
Graphic Design: Diana Patricia González Juárez
Copyright © 2024 Blas Antonio Herrera Pérez
ISBN Paperback: 978-1-68574-864-7
ISBN eBook: 978-1-68574-865-4

Table of Content

INTRODUCTION	5
CHAPTER 1 **THE PROBLEM**	9
CHAPTER 2 **THE INVESTMENT PLAN**	19
CHAPTER 3 **HOW WE WILL FINANCE IT**	21
THE ACTION PLAN	31
CALCULATIONS FOR FINANCING	33
CLARIFICATION	43

INTRODUCTION

My name is Blas Antonio Herrera Pérez. I was born in San Felipe, Edo. Yaracuy, on November 22, 1950. I graduated as an Electrical Engineer from the University of Carabobo. A few months before my academic graduation, I began working in the Venezuelan electrical sector (1972).

In 1974, I founded CIELEMCA C.A., a national private capital company, which entered the Venezuelan market to provide services in the engineering, procurement, and construction of projects for the National Electric System (SEN). We immediately began working for CADAFE within the Venezuelan Rural Electrification Project financed by the Inter-American Development Bank (IDB). This project was one of the most ambitious projects of the National Electric System (SEN) and was fully executed.

Under contracts with CIELEMCA C.A. and the KCT Consortium, led by CIELEMCA C.A., we worked for CADAFE, EDELCA, CORPOELEC, PDVSA Petróleo, and PDVSA Gas on projects of great importance.

Our achievements include 115/230/400 kV transmission and distribution lines that run through various states of the country, totaling 2,190 km. We completed the EPC of 200 MW of thermoelectric generation with dual generation units from General Electric (primary market), including one of the fourth installed in the world, the 100MW LMS, and the 103.5 MW generation barge we installed in San Lorenzo. We also executed the EPC of 16 electrical substations, 6 GIS type and 10 conventional, and installed 8 power transformers (30/36 MVA). Notably, we contributed to the National Electric System (SEN) by constructing over 7% of the 230/400 KV transmission system, utilizing Venezuelan labor that totaled just over 1,140,000 man-hours per year. (1)

The material I present to Venezuela today is the product of a new stage in my life—one where I reflect and seek solutions in light of the serious events occurring there. This is how the book "THINKING ABOUT VENEZUELA WITH ENERGY" was created. It aims to reflect and find solutions, proposing a progressive plan for the reconstruction of the National Electrical System (SEN), expressed in a series of strategic actions aimed at rescuing the electrical service for its inhabitants and all activists who wish to collaborate in the country's recovery.

There is no doubt that energy moves the world. Without electricity, there is no oil, no industrialization, no Internet, no development. Electricity is the foundation of other systems. We are talking about "critical infrastructure," which "includes essential and public utility facilities, systems, or services, as well as those whose impact causes serious damage to the health or supply of the population, to economic activity, to the environment, or to the security of the country" (2).

To avoid redundancy, I will not elaborate further on this topic. However, we are aware that the proposed reconstruction will take place in a unique environment, which requires careful analysis and understanding. Understanding the context of what is happening in our country requires developing a global vision, examining both the past and present. It necessitates scrutinizing and analyzing the systemic elements that contribute to the current situation.

It is undeniable that Venezuela faces an unprecedented economic, social, and political crisis. Some analysts define the situation "as a type of humanitarian crisis caused by the combination of various factors" (3). Others believe that "the humanitarian emergency affects almost a third of the population of Venezuela" (4) (OHCHR, UN Human Rights Office).

Now, history has its limits. It is useful for explaining how the country arrived at this point but not for guiding its future direction. Venezuela needs a country project defined with a long-term and systemic vision, where we evaluate all the components of the situation and their impact on the reconquest of our country and the electrical reconstruction project we intend to develop.

That is why we appeal to foresight. It constitutes a date with the future that, although full of visions and dreams, is rooted in reality, strategy, and action. It is not just about imagining and aspiring; it is about building. After forging a vision, we must construct it. As Concheiro wisely said: "He who renounces inventing futures becomes a slave to his history" (5).

Using my knowledge of the subject and my experience executing important works in the country, I propose to seek solutions. First, we must structure the problem, translating it into the question: How can we REBUILD the National Electrical System (SEN)? To answer this question, we start by generating a plan—defining, delimiting, organizing, and making it operational. We think strategically, visualizing a way out, and proposing short, medium, and long-term objectives and concrete actions. This is summarized in the document you have in your hands today.

To say goodbye, I want to express my emotions on behalf of the workers of CIELEMCA C.A. We are proud of our engineering contributions to the once prestigious National Electric System (SEN) of Venezuela. I fondly remember the unique harmony that existed between the energy supply provider and the energy consumer, and I am committed to rekindling the unforgettable camaraderie between the inhabitants of those popular neighborhoods and us. These memories stem from my early days as an engineer when I worked for Caracas's Electricity in a popular neighborhood of our capital. This way, we will contribute to enjoying Venezuela again, reminiscent of our old and improved times.

With this solid collaboration, I commit to continue working until Venezuela achieves its great natural potential, thanks to our immense natural wealth: crude oil, gold, silver, coltan, and above all, we Venezuelans, among others. We aim to revive the great Venezuela of hope and ensure, with absolute certainty, the return of the great

Venezuela of the future. I hope this is achieved with the contribution of all Venezuelans.

Your friend,
Blas Antonio Herrera Pérez

(1) (http://cieIemca.group/proyectos.html)

(2) In Venezuela, Vertigo and Future by Tanya Miquilena and Werner Corrales.

(3) Dictionary of Humanitarian Action and Development Cooperation, htto://)www.dicc.hegoa.ehu.es/listar/mostrar/85).

(4) The objectives of Sustainable Development in Venezuela (2019) by SINERGIA (Venezuelan Network of civil society organizations).

(5) Alonso Concheiro, in the prologue of the book PROSPECTIVE METHODS by Guillermo Gándara and Francisco Osorio.

CHAPTER 1
THE PROBLEM

According to the ISBL (Institute of Labor Safety and Welfare), CRITICAL INFRASTRUCTURES are defined as "all those physical or virtual systems that provide essential functions and services to support the most basic systems at a social, economic, environmental, and political level" (1). They further illustrate this with the following case: "An alteration or interruption in its operation due to natural causes (for example, a flood that affects the electricity supply) or caused by man (a terrorist attack or a cyber-attack on a nuclear power plant or a financial institution) could entail serious consequences" (2).

The critical infrastructure we will focus on in this document is electricity. Almost all of the strategic areas that underpin the functioning and development of each country depend on it, such as technological communications in general, banking, investments, reservoirs, storage, treatment and distribution of water, production, storage, and distribution of food, education, the chemical industry, research, health, transportation (airports, ports, railways, and public transportation networks, traffic control systems), and above all, the extraction of crude oil (petroleum).

When I think about this topic, there is a phrase of my own that I cannot fail to mention: "To extract a molecule of crude oil, it will always be necessary and sufficient for the protons and electrons to previously dance at the mouth of the extraction well."

In the opinion of experts, "a person is in a situation of poverty when their income does not allow them to survive and they have at least one social deficiency among the following indicators:

1. *Educational lag*
2. *Access to health services*
3. *Access to social security*
4. *Quality and spaces of the home*
5. *Basic services*
6. *Access to food"* (3)

Other sources of information assure that "about 860 million people in the world still lack access to electricity (2018)" (4). Not in vain, 94% (64% direct and 30% indirect) of the SDG (Sustainable Development Goals) of the 2030 UN Agenda have a vigorous relationship of support for the electrical service (5).

CHART 1
LINKAGE BETWEEN THE SDG AND THE ELECTRICAL SERVICE

A goal worthy of attention, at the time of preparing this document, is its alignment with the ECLAC 2030 Agenda. Sustainable development can only be achieved if the eradication of poverty and environmental sustainability go hand in hand. This means respecting the social foundations established as human rights and the environmental limits, known as "planetary limits." These boundaries are defined as "a safe space within which humanity can continue to develop for generations to come. Crossing these thresholds can generate acute and irreversible environmental changes" (6).

Now, I allow myself to introduce you to the Venezuelan Electrical System (SEN).

CHART 2
THE VENEZUELAN ELECTRICAL SYSTEM

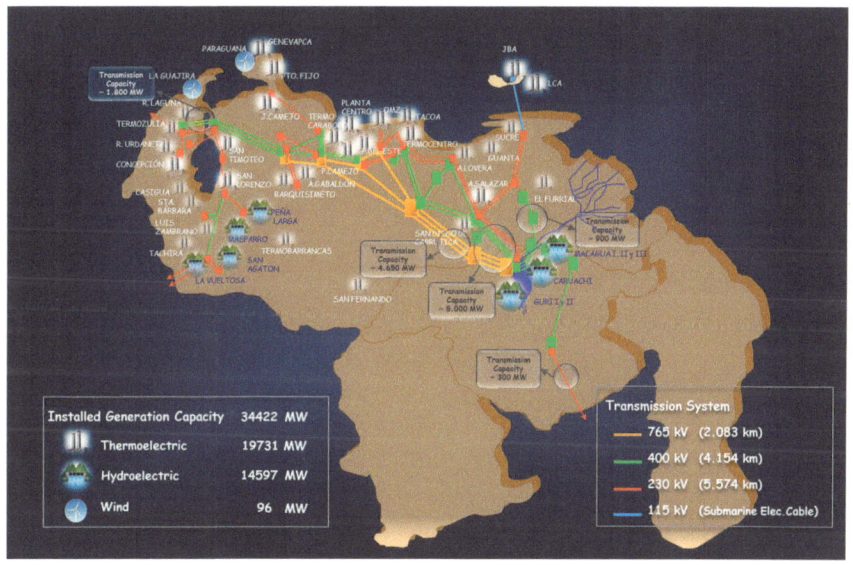

CHART 3
INSTALLED GENERATION CAPACITY (MW)

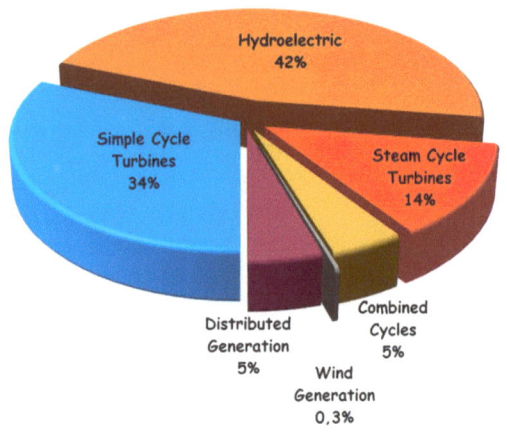

INSTALLED CAPACITY YEAR 2018	
Simple Cycle Turbines	11546 MW
Hydroelectric	14597 MW
Steam Cycle Turbines	4866 MW
Combined Cycles	1664 MW
Wind Generation	94 MW
Distributed Generation	1655 MW
Total	34422 MW

GRAPH 3 reveals in colors the portions that make up the installed capacity in 2018. As you can see, 42% corresponds to hydroelectric power, which was designed to cover 70% of the total need, in addition to the thermoelectric plant that was planned to ensure the remaining 30%, except on occasions when natural phenomena prevented it.

In this sense, diagnosing the Venezuelan situation regarding the electrical collapse and proposing a solution is a priority. What's more, Sustainable Development Goal (SDG) number 7 of the 2030 Agenda cites as the first desirable statistic, to determine its compliance, the index of "population that has access to electricity." This is how a 10-year project was designed that contemplates the necessary investment in electrical generation and transmission to improve the service and satisfy future increases.

With these ideas in mind, information was collected on the state of the main electrical installations, and their recovery was evaluated over a period of 20 years.

CHART 4
INSTALLED CAPACITY AND MAXIMUM DEMAND (MW)

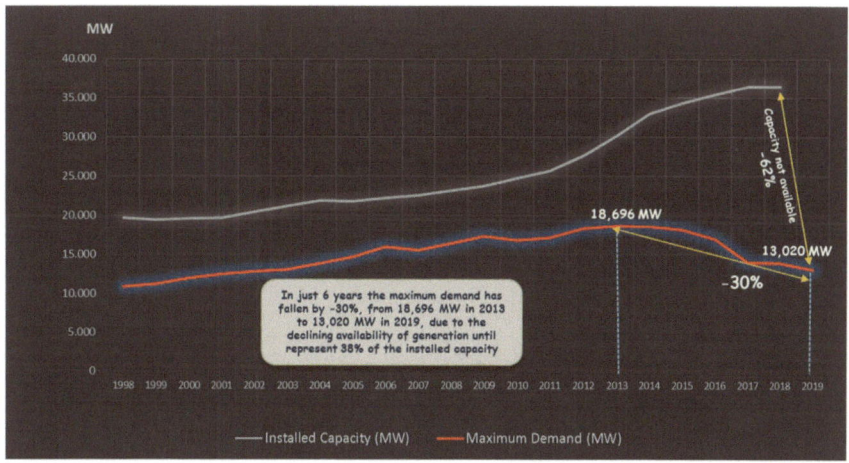

GRAPH 4 displays the path of the demand served over the course of 21 years, highlighting a sharp decrease of 30% in the period 2013-2019, from 18,696 MW in 2013 to 13,020 MW in 2019. This decline is mainly due to the decreased availability of electricity generation.

The comparative projection of the two curves in GRAPH 5 demonstrates the urgent need to undertake repairs and modifications in the electricity generation system. For thermoelectric generation, the main causes of unavailability are:

- Obsolescence of some generation units
- Lack of timely preventive and corrective maintenance
- Deficit of fuels, such as natural gas and diesel

In the case of hydroelectric generation, the main causes are:

- Obsolescence of some generation units
- Lack of timely preventive and corrective maintenance
- Deficiency in reservoir management during seasonal periods of rain and drought, as well as the extreme drought event known as "El Niño"

- Deficiency in the coordination for the dispatch of available thermoelectric generation and observance of the restrictive conditions of the transmission system (2)

CHART 5
PROJECTION OF REQUIRED GENERATION CAPACITY AND MAXIMUM DEMAND (MW)

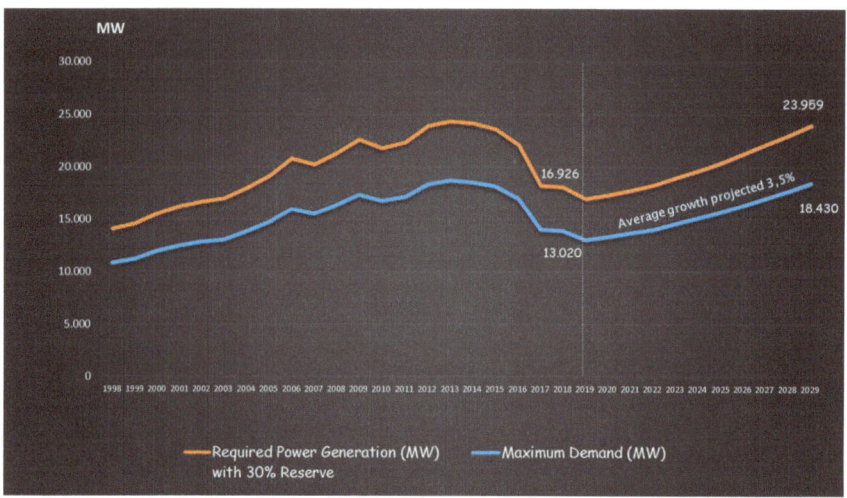

CHART 6
ANNUAL BEHAVIOR OF THE GURI
RESERVOIR LEVEL (1995-2016)

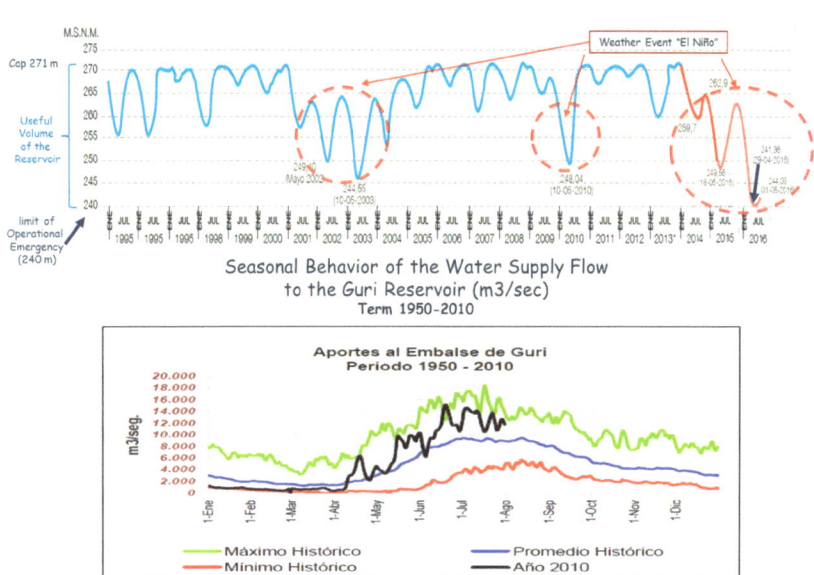

The previous image in GRAPH 6 shows the effects of the rains on the Guri reservoir, which is largely responsible for energy generation at the national level (76%). During severe droughts, such as those resulting from the "El Niño" phenomenon, the reservoir level can reach "Operational Emergency Limits," compromising the electricity supply.

"El Niño" or "Southern Oscillation" (ENSO) is a natural phenomenon characterized by the fluctuation of ocean temperatures in the central and eastern part of the equatorial Pacific, associated with atmospheric changes. This phenomenon significantly influences climatic conditions in various parts of the world. Its most intense manifestations cause havoc in the intertropical and equatorial zones due to intense rains, mainly affecting the Pacific coastal region of South America.

The lower part of GRAPH 6 represents the historical and seasonal behavior of the El Guri dam. It shows the water flow (m³/sec) that this reservoir has received for hydroelectric generation.

CHART 7
ENERGY REQUIREMENTS PROJECTION (GWh)

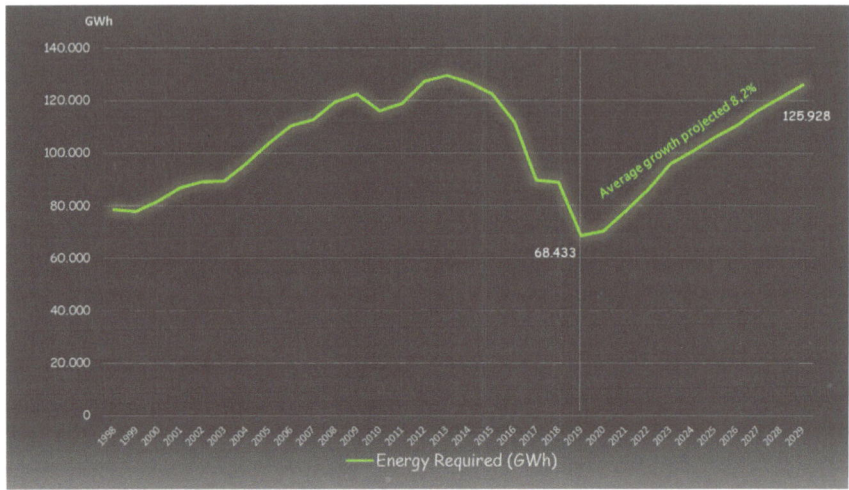

To achieve efficiency, the average annual growth in energy demand until 2029 was determined, as shown in GRAPH 7. It is important to clarify that this projection considers the gradual recovery of the national load factor, which has been affected by the decrease in the number of industries and businesses and their level of consumption, as well as the electricity rationing applied in recent years.

CHART 8
DISTRIBUTION OF GENERATED ENERGY (GWh)

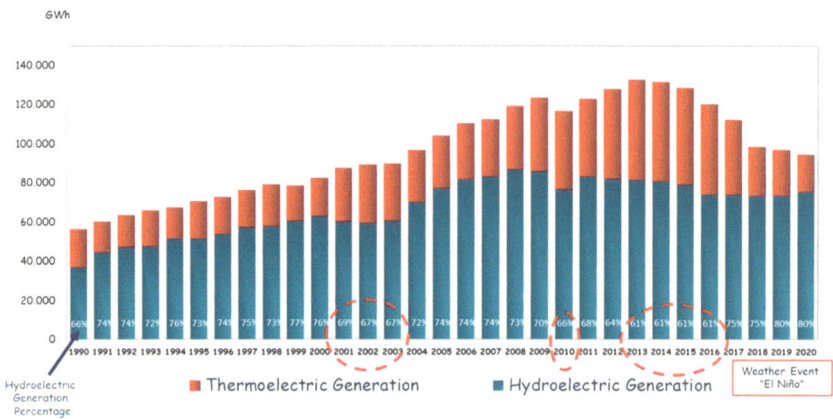

In GRAPH 8, referring to the Distribution of Generated Energy (GWh), it can be seen that between 1990 and 2020, hydroelectric energy generation was consistently higher than 70%, except for the years 2001-2003, 2010, and 2013-2016, due to the climatological event "El Niño." During the period 2013-2016, hydroelectric energy generation reached a minimum of 61%.

I reiterate that our National Electric System (SEN) is designed in an environmentally friendly manner, as long as the preventive maintenance of our hydroelectric generation units is rigorously respected, in accordance with the established protocol. This approach minimizes the need for corrective maintenance. By adhering to this standard, our thermoelectric generation will always be less than 30%.

It is important to remember that dual thermoelectric generation units from General Electric, such as the ones we installed in Bajo Grande (2 LM 50MW) and Morichal (1 LMS 100MW), practically do not produce gas emissions into the environment since the gas generated during their operation is reused.

Additionally, in a tropical country, we can always increase our generation of environmentally friendly electricity with wind and solar energy, among others.

As a result of the information gathering and analysis, two projects were generated: 90D-90S (emergency plan) and Plan 10 A, which covers future development. Prior to the execution of the emergency period, the first project contemplates the necessary investment in new electricity generation to satisfy the current increases in demand. The second project is based on information regarding the current state of electrical installations and their potential for long-term recovery.

I would like to remind you that our Oil Industry (PDVSA) once competed for leadership among the most prestigious oil companies in the world. We are the seed of OPEC, led by Juan Pablo Pérez Alfonso, and I am confident that we will become the flourishing plant that seed engendered. I feel very proud to be Venezuelan.

Quotes (1) and (2) extracted from https://isbi.eu/2020/03/que-son-las-infraestructuras-criticas/)

Quotes (3) and (5) extracted from Agenda 2030 of the Economic Commission for Latin America.

Quote (4) at https://www.acciona.com/es/energiasrenovables/?_adin=02021864894

Quote (6) https://www.cepal.org/sites/default/files/events/files/Christopher_dekki_desa.pdf)

Quote (6) Bengali poet (Rabindranath Tagore (1861 -1941)

CHAPTER 2
THE INVESTMENT PLAN

"Our greatest weakness lies in giving up. The surest way to succeed is to always try one more time"
Tomas Alva Edison

One of the flags in the rebellion against inequality waved by the socially and economically excluded is the absence of electricity. This absence manifests in lack of lighting, insufficient food preservation, poor health services, diminished education, inadequate transportation, and a myriad of other issues. The presence or absence of electricity has the power to change political groups, generate protests, exacerbate cultural marginalization, threaten health, and more.

On the other hand, ECLAC considers public services to include "transportation, communications, electricity, and water supply" (1). If I had prepared that list, it would be headed by electricity, as the other three depend partially or entirely on it. This service is crucial enough to tip the balance from the desired social equality and eradication of poverty decreed by the 2030 Agenda to evident inequality and the deprivation of access to fundamental human rights.

Obviously, we cannot give electricity the main role among services without losing the systemic and multidisciplinary perspective needed to address such a complex problem. However, we can acknowledge its privilege as the foundation of other essential services in our lives. It would be a mistake to work with a vision focused solely on the technical area because there is no way to separate the political system, the economic system, or these two from the social system. J. Marta Sosa reinforces these ideas by stating that inequality "bites into the cultural conditions of humanity and affects everyday political and institutional relations" (2).

Therefore, we will work by weighing the impact of each component on the project. We will need to learn new analytical languages, incorporate research tools, explore the ambitions of related groups, and maintain an open mind to consider findings from recent disciplines.

Without delving into philosophical depths that I do not dominate, I conceptualize equality as the right to have certain social structures that provide each individual with a starting platform to develop their natural capabilities, rather than comparing physical or intellectual characteristics between human beings.

David Eaton proposes that we "interpret political life... as a system of behaviors" to which we are irremediably linked (3). I make this quote because we are clear that, when starting the project, we will face multiple components with dissimilar, blurry, or debatable criteria. This will inevitably increase the complexity we already experience.

The general objective of this plan is to reconstruct the National Electric System (SEN), with four subordinate objectives:

- Protect existing facilities.
- Reduce the electricity generation deficit by addressing the increase in demand.
- Take operational, technical, and financial control of the National Electrical Transmission System, with the participation of the Venezuelan State as shareholders in accordance with the current value agreed upon by the parties participating in the financing of the recovery of the National Electrical System (SEN).
- Guarantee future oil production.

(1) Quote taken from the 2030 Agenda of the Economic Commission for Latin America.

(2) Quote from Joaquín Marta Sosa.

(3) Quote taken from Outline for Political Analysis by David Eaton.

CHAPTER 3
HOW WE WILL FINANCE IT

Today, managers must solve truly complicated problems and situations because they are made up of multiple factors and systemic relationships that make it difficult to move forward with accurate actions. In this sense, it is important to see the future with energy and positive force supported by our knowledge, generating an atmosphere of optimism that leads us to obtain the developed country that all Venezuelans desire.

The scenario we will face when beginning the reconstruction of the National Electric System (SEN) is both complex and uncertain; this is the environment in which we must work. We will challenge dynamic and volatile contexts, moving from a present state to a desired one. To do this, we will require great analytical capacity, resources, goodwill, and love for the country. We are prepared for this situation.

It is obvious that we have relied on structural models of problem analysis, which ensure that "hard systemic thinking involves starting from a carefully defined objective" (1). It is also evident that we do not have recent information. The consequence of using an outdated base is clear: there will be **learning and findings, supported by knowledge and experience.** However, articulating the process will allow room for reorganization and creativity.

The preceding reflection is relevant when we think about how we will finance such an enormous project, because we are talking about billions of dollars. The word "negotiation" translates into the need to sit at the table, confront the different positions of the members, rethink the facts, evaluate the results, and **make concessions.** As a result of these reflections, the wise words of Neufville and Keeney (1972) come to mind: "Great decisions are not made by a single group of experts… they are, rather, the result of negotiations, explicit or implicit, between representatives of different points of view" (2).

Sociologists claim that life in society would not be possible if perceptions and evaluations did not overlap to some extent. Let's take advantage of that to form an organization with a single purpose: to rebuild the SEN. We understand that the agreement will not be complete, but we intend to subject disagreements to adjustments within the required area.

Let's talk now about which organizations can help us rebuild the SEN.

One potential partner is the World Bank Group, which comprises the International Bank for Reconstruction and Development (IBRD), the International Development Association (IDA), the International Finance Corporation (IFC), the Multilateral Investment Guarantee Agency (MIGA), and the International Center for Settlement of Investment Disputes (ICSID). This organization is one of the main international sources of financing and knowledge for developing countries. The five institutions that comprise it have a common commitment to reducing poverty, increasing prosperity, and promoting sustainable development. Through these foundations, the World Bank Group provides financing, technical assistance, political risk insurance, and solutions to private businesses, including financial institutions (3).

Another alternative is the International Monetary Fund (IMF). "The IMF is an organization made up of 184 countries. It is headquartered in Washington, DC, United States. Its main objective is to grant credits to member countries experiencing difficulties in their balance of payments, so they can carry out reforms and adjustments aimed at solving the problems caused by a crisis" (4).

I mention below some of the countries to which the IMF has granted loans: Germany, Australia, Belgium, Finland, Brazil, Portugal, Morocco, Canada, China, Iceland, Ireland, South Korea, Spain, France, Italy, Thailand, Peru, Paraguay, Argentina, Guatemala, Mexico, Venezuela, and 164 more listed in the registry. What I want to make clear is that we will not be the first or the most recent to request help of this nature.

Many of these processes have been real and successful, managing to recover from acute economic crises and achieve their current prosperity. One notable example is Iceland, which is currently experiencing a golden age. However, in 2008, it suffered a total collapse due to the real estate bubble in the United States. As a result of the financial situation, Lehman Brothers Bank went bankrupt, triggering panic among the population. Icelandic banks went bankrupt because they had to repay the money they borrowed, leading them to liquidate their assets in krona to pay in dollars or euros. The Icelandic currency lost 85% of its value, and external debt at that time was 32 times greater than the foreign exchange reserves in the Icelandic Central Bank.

In response, and supported by Emergency Law No. 15/2008, the Icelandic government nationalized the banking system and cut non-financial public spending by 12.7%. The United Kingdom also froze remaining assets to support debt repayment. The outlook seemed dire. At that time, the Icelandic government sought help from the IMF and other countries to face the crisis. Today, Iceland enjoys great prosperity (5).

Another notable case was the Irish crisis (2008–2013), a major political and financial crisis considered by experts to be partially responsible for the country's fall into recession for the first time since the 1980s. In September 2008, the Irish government officially recognized that the country had entered recession, with a severe rise in unemployment occurring in the following months. In fact, it was the first state in the eurozone to suffer from it, as declared by the Central Statistics Office.

On November 21, 2010, the State confirmed that Ireland had formally requested financial assistance from the European Financial Stability Facility (EFSF) of the European Union and the International Monetary Fund (IMF), and they had reached an agreement for an amount of €85 billion. The 2011 general elections replaced one political trend with another. However, the newly arrived team continued with the same austerity measures as the previous government, united with the largest parties in the country, in support of a single agenda. In

2013, Ireland officially emerged from the bailout. According to a government representative's speech, the country was moving in the right direction, and the economy was beginning to recover (6).

Let's reflect a little on why crises occur.

The causes of crises are varied and complex. They can arise from **internal or external factors. Domestic factors** could include the implementation of inadequate fiscal and monetary policies, which lead to large fiscal deficits and significant public debt. Additionally, exchange rates fixed at inappropriate levels can erode competitiveness and lead to the loss of official reserves, while a weak financial system can generate cycles of boom and bust in the economy. Political instability and weak institutions can also trigger a crisis.

External factors include unexpected events such as the COVID-19 pandemic, natural disasters like floods, prolonged droughts, or earthquakes, and strong fluctuations in raw material prices. All of these factors pose a significant threat, especially in low-income countries. Moreover, globalization, with its abrupt changes, can erode market confidence, causing volatility in capital flows.

Now, what kind of help does the IMF provide to a country in crisis?

The IMF provides loans and technical advice to countries experiencing difficulties, allowing them to adjust their policies in an orderly manner. This helps lay the foundations for a stable economy and sustainable growth. Policy adjustments will vary depending on the circumstances. For example, a country facing a sudden drop in the price of key export products may need financial assistance while it takes steps to strengthen its economy and diversify its exports.

Another issue could be a serious capital flight caused by factors such as interest rates that are too low, privatization of private entities, excessive socioeconomic assistance policies, budget deficits, or an inefficient or poorly regulated banking system. To address these difficulties, the IMF provides financing through a gradual adjustment, usually accompanied by a series of corrective measures that encourage the return of private investors.

IMF loans also aim to protect the most vulnerable population by including conditions related to economic policy. In low-income countries, loans often channel financial support from other donors and development partners.

The IMF lending process is flexible. Countries that maintain a commitment to the implementation of solid policies can access resources without conditionality or with limited conditionality. The same applies to certain urgent and immediate needs covered by emergency financing instruments.

However, we must not lose sight of the fact that we are not the object of someone's charity; we are engaging in a business. So, the correct question to ask is:

What type of guarantees does the lender require?

The IMF has several lending instruments that meet the different needs and specific circumstances of its member countries. These countries have access to the General Resources Account (GRA), currently at zero interest rates, or through the Growth and Development Trust Fund and the Fight Against Poverty (FFCLP), which is better adapted to the diversity and needs of low-income countries. But, as with any negotiation, countries must **guarantee the repayment of the loan and return the borrowed capital.** To do so, they use the monetary, physical, or natural resources at their disposal.

The question that immediately arises is: What assets does Venezuela possess to guarantee the return of the money? Without much thought, I affirm that: the crude oil that rests in the subsoil and our National Electrical System, once completely recovered and repowered, can serve as guarantees.

I want to tell you about some cases I remember of countries that, in the middle of a crisis, had to seek international monetary support. In 2010, Honduras requested a loan of 200 million dollars from the Inter-American Development Bank (IDB) and put its electrical system as collateral. Another example was Nicaragua in 2014, which obtained 60 million dollars from the European Investment Bank (EIB).

In 2018, both El Salvador and Jamaica used the same strategy to secure loans of 170 million dollars from the Central American Bank for Economic Integration (CABEI) and 40 million dollars from the World Bank (WB), respectively (7).

Obviously, using the electrical system as collateral to obtain financing can have significant implications for the economy and the population. Therefore, we will evaluate this measure carefully and in consultation with the corresponding authorities. In my opinion, using the electrical system as a guarantee to obtain financing would enhance the development of the Action Plan, with an immediate impact on our economy, which is characterized by abundant natural resources, led by our oil reserves. This approach would align us with international financial markets and at the same time allow for economic participation in the company that would be created for such purposes.

Chile, for example, uses a different strategy as a debtor to the IMF. It focuses on the production of Green Hydrogen, which is associated with renewable sources. To obtain it, they rely on three great assets: solar radiation in the Atacama Desert, strong winds in the extreme south of the country convertible into wind energy, and the enormous coastal property that provides opportunities to produce tidal and hydroelectric energy. According to 2021 Chilean government estimates, 13% of the world's green hydrogen could potentially be produced using wind energy from Magallanes and the Chilean portion of Antarctica, totaling 126 gigawatts. In summary, Chile has the potential to be one of the most efficient and competitive producers of green hydrogen in the world (8).

Now let's talk specifically about Venezuela's crude oil reserves, using figures shown in two important reports:

The first report comes from British Petroleum, one of the largest companies in the world dedicated to oil and natural gas, based in the United Kingdom (London). In CHART 9, it can be seen that our country occupied first place in 2020 in crude oil reserves, expressed in billions of barrels (9).

CHART 9
TOTAL PROVED RESERVES

Oil
Total proved reserves

	At end 2000 Thousand million barrels	At end 2010 Thousand million barrels	At end 2019 Thousand million barrels	At end 2020 Thousand million barrels	At end 2020 Thousand million tonnes	Share of total	R/P ratio
Canada	181.5	174.8	169.1	168.1	27.1	9.7%	89.4
Mexico	24.6	10.4	6.1	6.1	0.9	0.4%	8.7
US	30.4	35.0	68.8	68.8	8.2	4.0%	11.4
Total North America	236.5	220.2	244.0	242.9	36.1	14.0%	28.7
Argentina	3.0	2.5	2.5	2.5	0.3	0.1%	11.3
Brazil	8.5	14.2	12.7	11.9	1.7	0.7%	10.8
Colombia	2.0	1.9	2.0	2.0	0.3	0.1%	7.1
Ecuador	2.7	2.1	1.3	1.3	0.2	0.1%	7.4
Peru	0.9	1.2	0.8	0.7	0.1	*	15.5
Trinidad & Tobago	0.9	0.8	0.2	0.2	†	*	8.7
Venezuela	76.8	296.5	303.8	303.8	48.0	17.5%	*
Other S. & Cent. America	1.3	0.8	0.7	0.8	0.1	*	10.9
Total S. & Cent. America	96.0	320.1	324.0	323.4	50.8	18.7%	161.9
Denmark	1.1	0.9	0.4	0.4	0.1	*	16.2
Italy	0.6	0.6	0.6	0.6	0.1	*	14.7
Norway	11.4	6.8	8.5	7.9	1.0	0.5%	10.8
Romania	1.2	0.6	0.6	0.6	0.1	*	22.7
United Kingdom	4.7	2.8	2.5	2.5	0.3	0.1%	6.6
Other Europe	2.1	1.9	1.6	1.6	0.2	0.1%	14.9
Total Europe	21.1	13.6	14.2	13.6	1.8	0.8%	10.4
Azerbaijan	1.2	7.0	7.0	7.0	1.0	0.4%	26.7
Kazakhstan	5.4	30.0	30.0	30.0	3.9	1.7%	45.3
Russian Federation	112.1	105.8	107.8	107.8	14.8	6.2%	27.6
Turkmenistan	0.5	0.6	0.6	0.6	0.1	*	7.6
Uzbekistan	0.6	0.6	0.6	0.6	0.1	*	34.7
Other CIS	0.3	0.3	0.3	0.3	†	*	17.3
Total CIS	120.1	144.2	146.2	146.2	19.9	8.4%	29.0
Iran	99.5	151.2	157.8	157.8	21.7	9.1%	139.8
Iraq	112.5	115.0	145.0	145.0	19.6	8.4%	96.3
Kuwait	96.5	101.5	101.5	101.5	14.0	5.9%	103.2
Oman	5.8	5.5	5.4	5.4	0.7	0.3%	15.4
Qatar	16.9	24.7	25.2	25.2	2.6	1.5%	38.1
Saudi Arabia	262.8	264.5	297.6	297.5	40.9	17.2%	73.6
Syria	2.3	2.5	2.5	2.5	0.3	0.1%	158.8
United Arab Emirates	97.8	97.8	97.8	97.8	13.0	5.6%	73.1
Yemen	2.4	3.0	3.0	3.0	0.4	0.2%	86.7
Other Middle East	0.2	0.2	0.2	0.2	†	*	2.6
Total Middle East	696.7	765.9	836.0	835.9	113.2	48.3%	82.2
Algeria	11.3	12.2	12.2	12.2	1.5	0.7%	25.0
Angola	6.0	9.1	7.8	7.8	1.1	0.4%	16.1
Chad	0.9	1.5	1.5	1.5	0.2	0.1%	32.5
Republic of Congo	1.6	2.0	2.9	2.9	0.4	0.2%	25.7
Egypt	3.6	4.5	3.1	3.1	0.4	0.2%	14.0
Equatorial Guinea	0.6	1.7	1.1	1.1	0.1	0.1%	19.7
Gabon	2.4	2.0	2.0	2.0	0.3	0.1%	28.4
Libya	36.0	47.1	48.4	48.4	6.3	2.8%	339.2
Nigeria	29.0	37.2	36.9	36.9	5.0	2.1%	56.1
South Sudan	n/a	n/a	3.5	3.5	0.5	0.2%	56.4
Sudan	0.3	5.0	1.5	1.5	0.2	0.1%	47.9
Tunisia	0.4	0.4	0.4	0.4	0.1	*	32.7
Other Africa	0.7	2.3	3.7	3.8	0.5	0.2%	13.2
Total Africa	93.8	124.8	125.0	125.1	16.6	7.2%	49.6
Australia	4.8	3.0	2.4	2.4	0.3	0.1%	13.9
Brunei	1.1	1.1	1.1	1.1	0.1	0.1%	27.3
China	15.2	23.3	26.0	26.0	3.5	1.5%	18.2
India	5.3	5.8	4.7	4.5	0.6	0.3%	16.1
Indonesia	5.1	4.2	2.5	2.4	0.3	0.1%	9.0
Malaysia	2.1	3.6	2.7	2.7	0.4	0.2%	12.5
Thailand	0.5	0.4	0.3	0.3	†	*	1.7
Vietnam	2.0	4.4	4.4	4.4	0.6	0.3%	58.1
Other Asia Pacific	1.3	1.1	1.4	1.3	0.2	0.1%	17.4
Total Asia Pacific	37.7	47.0	45.3	45.2	6.1	2.6%	16.6
Total World	**1300.9**	**1636.9**	**1734.8**	**1732.4**	**244.4**	**100.0%**	**53.5**
of which: OECD	267.7	238.5	261.5	260.0	38.3	15.0%	25.2
Non-OECD	1033.2	1398.3	1473.3	1472.4	206.1	85.0%	66.9
OPEC	833.0	1137.2	1214.7	1214.7	171.8	70.1%	108.3
Non-OPEC	468.0	499.1	520.1	517.7	72.6	29.9%	24.5
European Union	3.9	3.2	2.4	2.4	0.3	0.1%	16.8
Canadian oil sands: Total	174.9	169.2	162.4	161.4	26.2	9.3%	
of which: Under active development	11.7	25.9	19.9	18.9	3.1	1.1%	
Venezuela: Orinoco Belt		220.0	261.8	261.8	42.0	15.1%	

Source of data: the estimates in this table have been compiled using a combination of primary official sources, third-party data from the OPEC Secretariat, World Oil, Oil & Gas Journal and Chinese reserves based on official data and information in the public domain.
† Less than 0.05.
* Less than 0.05%.
n/a not available
◊ More than 100 years

Additionally, CHART 10 issued by the Organization of Petroleum Exporting Countries (OPEC) also confirms this information for the year 2021.

CHART 10
WORLD PROVEN CRUDE OIL RESERVES BY COUNTRY
(Annual Statistical Bulletin 2021)

Oil data: upstream

Table 3.1
World proven crude oil reserves by country (mb)

	2017	2018	2019	2020	2021	% change 21/20
OECD Americas	51,270	54,973	54,580	46,488	49,605	6.7
Canada[1]	5,423	5,192	4,906	5,005	5,005	0.0
Chile	150	150	150	150	150	0.0
Mexico	6,537	5,807	5,333	5,498	5,618	2.2
United States	39,160	43,824	44,191	35,835	38,832	8.4
OECD Europe	12,454	13,098	13,224	12,412	11,552	-6.9
Denmark	439	428	441	441	428	-2.9
Norway	7,918	8,645	8,523	7,902	7,525	-4.8
United Kingdom	2,500	2,500	2,700	2,500	2,000	-20.0
Others	1,597	1,525	1,560	1,569	1,599	1.9
OECD Asia and Pacific	2,493	2,483	2,477	2,475	1,833	-25.9
Australia	2,390	2,390	2,390	2,390	1,747	-26.9
Others	103	93	87	85	86	1.2
China	25,627	25,927	26,154	26,023	26,491	1.8
India	4,495	4,423	4,423	4,605	3,670	-20.3
Other Asia	13,583	13,415	13,577	12,841	12,829	-0.1
Brunei	1,100	1,100	1,100	1,100	1,100	0.0
Indonesia	3,310	3,170	3,150	2,480	2,440	-1.6
Malaysia	3,600	3,600	3,600	3,600	3,600	0.0
Vietnam	4,400	4,400	4,400	4,400	4,400	0.0
Others	1,173	1,145	1,327	1,261	1,289	2.2
Latin America	329,283	330,461	331,628	330,719	329,481	-0.4
Argentina	2,162	2,017	2,389	2,483	2,411	-2.9
Brazil	12,634	12,835	13,435	12,715	11,890	-6.5
Colombia	1,665	1,782	1,960	2,036	1,820	-10.6
Ecuador	8,273	8,273	8,273	8,273	8,273	0.0
Venezuela	302,809	303,806	303,806	303,561	303,468	0.0
Others	1,740	1,748	1,765	1,651	1,619	-1.9
Middle East	804,639	803,184	863,418	865,519	869,612	0.5
IR Iran	155,600	155,600	208,600	208,600	208,600	0.0
Iraq	147,223	145,019	145,019	145,019	145,019	0.0
Kuwait	101,500	101,500	101,500	101,500	101,500	0.0
Oman	5,373	5,373	5,373	5,373	5,373	0.0
Qatar	25,244	25,244	25,244	25,244	25,244	0.0
Saudi Arabia	266,260	267,026	267,073	267,082	267,192	0.0
Syrian Arab Republic	2,500	2,500	2,500	2,500	2,500	0.0
United Arab Emirates	97,800	97,800	105,000	107,000	111,000	3.7
Others	3,139	3,122	3,109	3,201	3,184	-0.5
Africa	127,677	126,972	125,228	124,560	120,210	-3.5
Algeria	12,200	12,200	12,200	12,200	12,200	0.0
Angola	8,384	8,160	7,783	7,231	2,516	-65.2
Congo	2,982	2,982	1,947	1,811	1,811	0.0
Egypt	3,325	3,325	3,075	3,075	3,300	7.3
Equatorial Guinea	1,100	1,100	1,100	1,100	1,100	0.0
Gabon	2,000	2,000	2,000	2,000	2,000	0.0
Libya	48,363	48,363	48,363	48,363	48,363	0.0
Nigeria	37,453	36,972	36,890	36,910	37,050	0.4
Sudans	5,000	5,000	5,000	5,000	5,000	0.0
Others	6,870	6,870	6,870	6,870	6,870	0.0
Russia	80,000	80,000	80,000	80,000	80,000	0.0
Other Eurasia	38,874	38,874	38,874	38,874	38,874	0.0
Azerbaijan	7,000	7,000	7,000	7,000	7,000	0.0
Belarus	198	198	198	198	198	0.0
Kazakhstan	30,000	30,000	30,000	30,000	30,000	0.0
Turkmenistan	600	600	600	600	600	0.0
Ukraine	395	395	395	395	395	0.0
Uzbekistan	594	594	594	594	594	0.0
Others	87	87	87	87	87	0.0
Other Europe	932	932	914	914	914	0.0
Total world	**1,491,327**	**1,494,742**	**1,554,497**	**1,545,430**	**1,545,071**	**0.0**
of which						
OPEC	1,183,674	1,182,528	1,241,281	1,242,377	1,241,819	0.0
OPEC percentage	79.4	79.1	79.9	80.4	80.4	
OECD	66,217	70,554	70,281	61,375	62,990	2.6

Notes: Figures as at year-end
1. Data excludes oil sands.

It is also important to take into account the potential of Venezuela in terms of its oil production for more than sixty years, as can be seen in CHART 11.

CHART 11

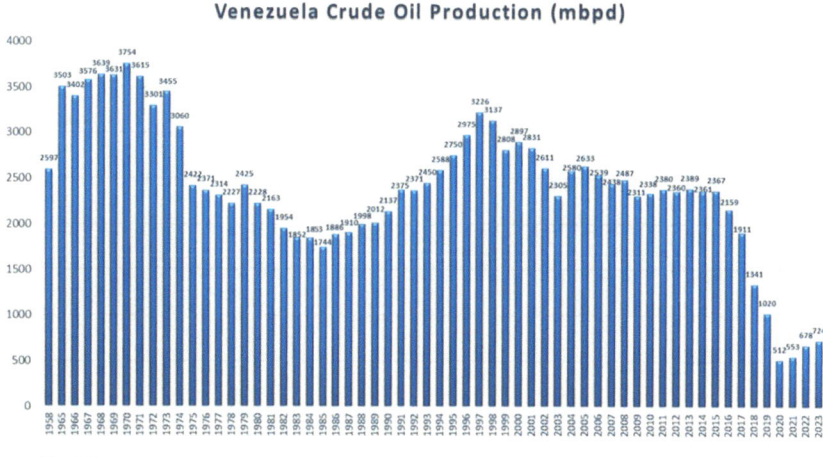

In addition to production, income from oil exports was recorded, as seen in CHART 12, which is also influenced by the variations in oil prices shown in CHART 13.

CHART 12

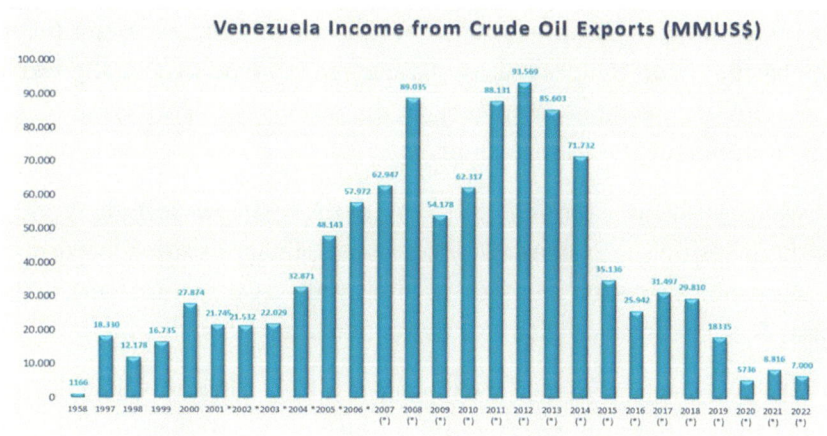

CHART 13
Why start Venezuela's recovery by giving priority to the national electrical system?

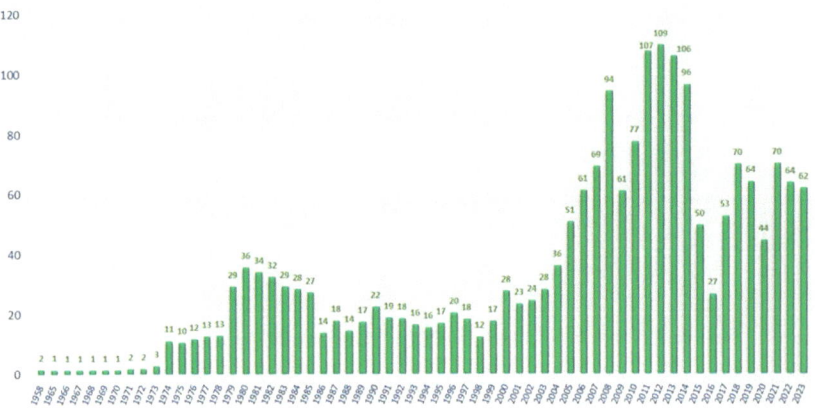

CEPAL considers "transportation, communications, electricity, and water supply" as public services. If I had prepared that list, it would be headed by electricity since the rest of the services depend partially or totally on it. The infrastructure we prioritize weighs enough to tip the balance from the desired social equality and eradication of poverty (Year 2030) to evident inequality, in the face of the deprivation of access to fundamental human rights.

Obviously, we cannot give electricity the main role among services without losing the systemic and multidisciplinary position needed to face a problem of such complexity. However, we can assure that it is the basis or foundation of the most fundamental services.

One of the flags in the rebellion against inequality waved by the socially and economically excluded is the lack of electrical current, which results in the deprivation of lighting, food, health, education, transportation, and other necessities. Its existence or nonexistence affects political, economic, and social life.

However, we cannot work with an encapsulated vision focused solely on the technical area because there is no way to separate the political system, the economic system, or these two from the social system. We will work by weighing the impact of each component on the project, learning new analytical languages, incorporating research tools, exploring the ambitions of related groups, and opening ourselves to findings from recent disciplines.

Without delving into philosophical depths, I conceptualize equality as the right to have certain social structures that provide individuals with a starting platform to develop their natural capabilities, and not as a comparison of physical or intellectual characteristics between human beings.

We are clear that, when starting the project, we will have to face multiple components with dissimilar, blurry criteria or debatable limits. This will inevitably increase the complexity that is already experienced. Faced with such a contingency, a negotiating table will be created, and the possibilities to recover our electrical assets will be explored.

In any case, it is time to look for solutions, doing what is necessary and sufficient to make them a reality. It is time to get "to work" and execute the recovery of the SEN. Regarding this topic, Savater had an expression that I fully share: "To change the world, you have to be optimistic. Pessimists are those who think that we cannot move a stone or that they will not let us move it" (11).

I am in the first group.

THE ACTION PLAN

For the design of the Action Plan, information was collected on the current state of the electrical installations and their potential for recovery. Aware of the absence of a "hard environment," we proceeded to define the problem with two types of content: the most recent information collected and the projection of this data into the future. This approach aims to propose solutions that provide short-term operability and reliability of the electrical service. Based on these ideas, we obtained an outline of the Action Plan.

Before presenting the following graphs, I want to refer to the outdated data used to prepare them. Despite the lack of up-to-date information, processing this data has allowed us to generate projections and calculations, from which we derived activities, costs, and execution times.

The first optimistic thought that mitigates this obstacle is that within the accepted uncertainty, we will have complementary and reliable data. I am referring to the data from the machinery and the parts that make it up, which "are considered systems with a tendency to balance, having a purpose defined by their designer" (12). This means they generate a type of **predictable behavior**, as they tend to move in a known direction.

The second factor in our favor focuses on the method with which the project was developed. Among a group of qualified professionals, we have built over the years a shared vision of the needs of our Venezuelan electrical system. We are aware of the useful life of each part, have a clear knowledge of how each unit operates and its importance within the whole, and have expert personnel to replace it. Additionally, since we have contacts with the companies that supply these parts, we can estimate how long it will take them to arrive in Venezuela, we have been informed of their current cost, and we have estimated a global figure to execute the project. We also have a clear idea of how we will finance it.

It is obvious that we are faced with limiting factors, such as lack of maintenance or climatic variations. However, these inconveniences are also **foreseeable factors,** which we will combat with vigor and assertiveness. In summary, whatever the time and place in which the work is carried out, we will assume it with confidence. We have a meticulous plan, our criteria, and experience, which opens up a range of possibilities for eliminating components we have deemed very important or including those that have been revalued according to the circumstances and are decisive for solving the problem.

J. M. García reinforces this idea by correctly commenting that in recent history, more and more limitations of the scientific method appear when it comes to applying a "reductionist approach," given the complexity of current problems. He concludes that "we cannot always obtain exhaustive knowledge" (13) because we work in open environments.

I close this clarification with the reflections of the philosopher Joan-Carles Mélich: "Dare to exist without firm and secure truths; in the indeterminacy, in the uncertainty, in the ambiguity of the world. Fragility is the relationship we establish with the world, and at any moment it can be broken" (14).

CALCULATIONS FOR FINANCING

After deciding to share our financing model with all Venezuelans, we will present graphics from the PowerPoint presentation created for this purpose, starting with the projection of the annualized costs of the fuels to be consumed over the next 20 years. In this projection, fuel consumption for the second decade was considered with a growth rate in accordance with the future electricity demand and the use of natural gas for new electricity generation.

It is worth mentioning that the projection of annual costs for fuel consumption is based on a progressive increase in prices, reaching objective values similar to the average prices in the USA as of July 2019 (Energy Information Administration - EIA) by the fifth year of the financing model:

Natural Gas = 1.38 USD/MMBTU

Diesel = 0.463 USD/lt = 74.07 USD/b

Fuel Oil= 0.315 USD/lt = 45.53 USD/b

Starting in the sixth year, a price increase of 3% per year was considered. The result is shown in CHART 14.

CHART 14
PROJECTION OF ANNUAL FUELS COSTS

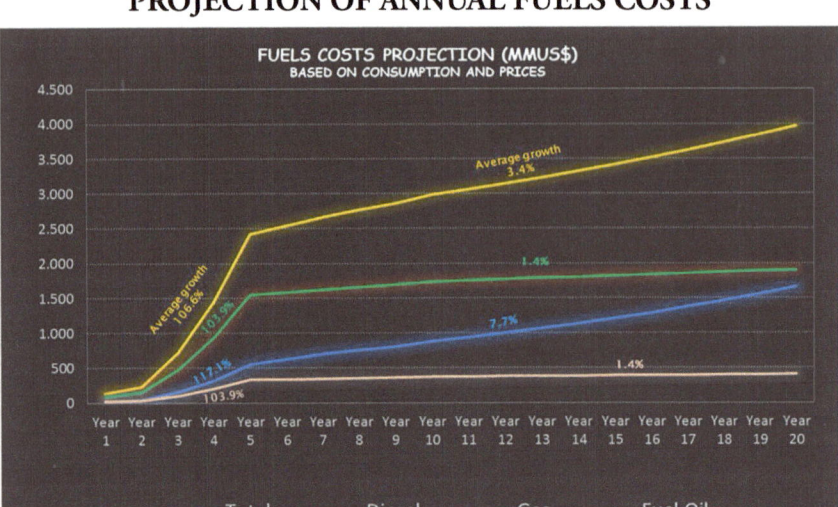

We intend that through the income produced by fuels, we will quickly reverse the current unavailability rates to offer, in the medium term, an operational and reliable electrical service in each of the areas: generation, transmission, distribution, and marketing. The first phase will be carried out in 90 days (urgent) and the second in 90 weeks (medium term). We call this project PLAN 90D-90S.

The third phase, planned for 10 years (PLAN-10A), contemplates the investment necessary to satisfy the future requirements of electricity demand, based on its historical behavior over the last 20 years, with an average growth rate of 3.5%.

As a result of these considerations, we conclude that, to satisfy the demand in 2029, a generation availability of around 24,000 MW is required. This takes into account a generation reserve criterion of 30% to account for scheduled and forced maintenance of the electrical generation units. (See CHART 15)

CHART 15
PROJECTION OF DEMAND AND
ELECTRICAL GENERATION (MW)

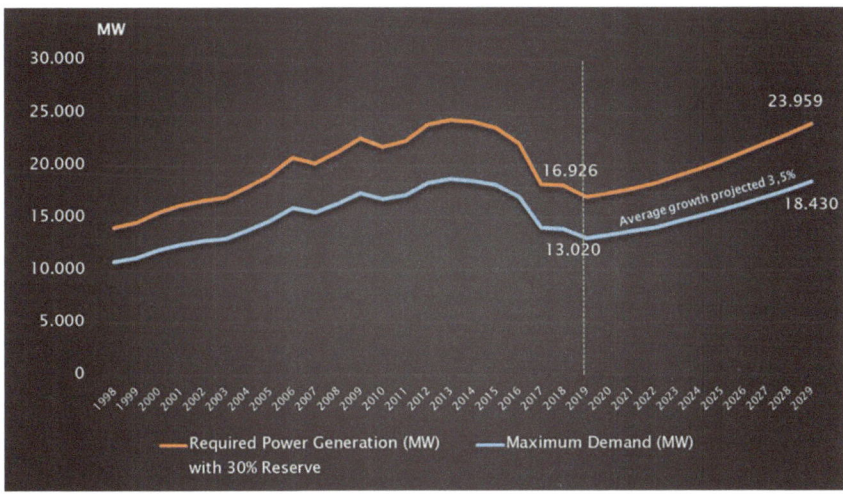

According to the expected energy generation for each year, the fuel consumption of the existing generation units (Natural Gas, Diesel, and Fuel Oil) was determined in relation to their historical spending patterns. This was based on the commissioning of the units according to the planning stipulated for the first decade. For the projection of the second decade, it was assumed that the growth rate would be associated with the growth of electricity demand and the increased use of natural gas for new generation.

To determine the income from electricity sales, we used the consumption structure of Venezuela in 2013 and the energy demand projection shown earlier. We then made a progressive adjustment of the current rate levels until they reach values close to the corresponding rates in South America, according to the CIER 2013 report. The objective is to ensure that income from electricity sales makes the Plan sustainable, as shown in CHART 16 below.

CHART 16
ELECTRICAL RATES PROJECTION (US$/kWh)

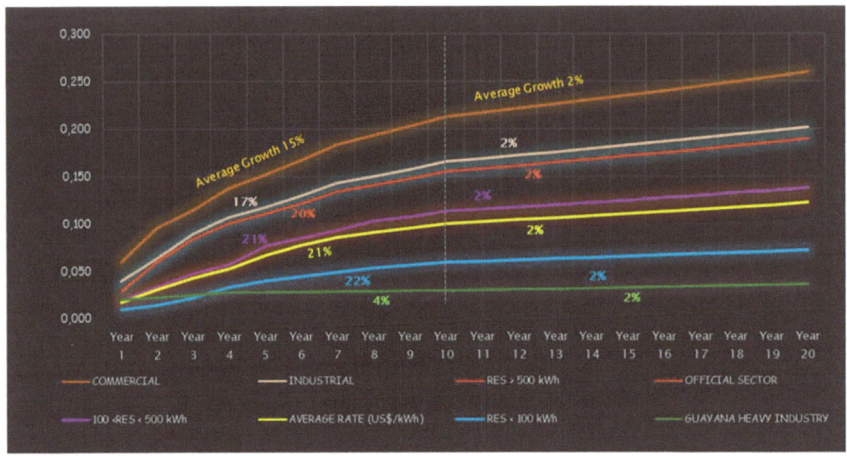

With the projection of electricity rates and sales by consumer sector, the income projection for the 20-year period is thus obtained.

CHART 18 defines the types of consumers by sector: Official (9%), Industrial (7%), Heavy Industry (2%), Commercial (9%), Technical Losses (12%), Non-Technical Losses (28%), and shows the structure of electricity consumption that we have foreseen in our financing model for a period of 20 years.

From CHART 18, we can see that the energy consumption for the first year amounts to 57,028 GWh (2018), the year in which the model was generated. This consumption is estimated to rise to 120,977 GWh in year 10 and 148,465 GWh in year 20. It is noteworthy that non-technical energy losses, quantified at 28% for the first year, are projected to be reduced to 1%.

The same graph shows the structure of income from electricity sales. For year 1, an income of 998.97 million USD was estimated, rising to 12,113.22 million USD in year 10, and up to an estimated income of 17,086.90 million USD in year 20.

It is important to highlight that residential clients with a consumption of less than 100 kWh per month, estimated in the structure at

5%, will receive a subsidy during year 1 for 50% of these clients. That percentage will drop to 30% in year 10 and to 0% in year 20.

The abbreviation RES identifies the residential population sector, which is divided into three groups: those who consume less than 100 kWh per month, those who consume between 100 kWh and 500 kWh per month, and those who consume more than 500 kWh per month.

**CHART 17
CONSUMPTION AND INCOME FROM
ELECTRICITY SALES BY SECTOR**

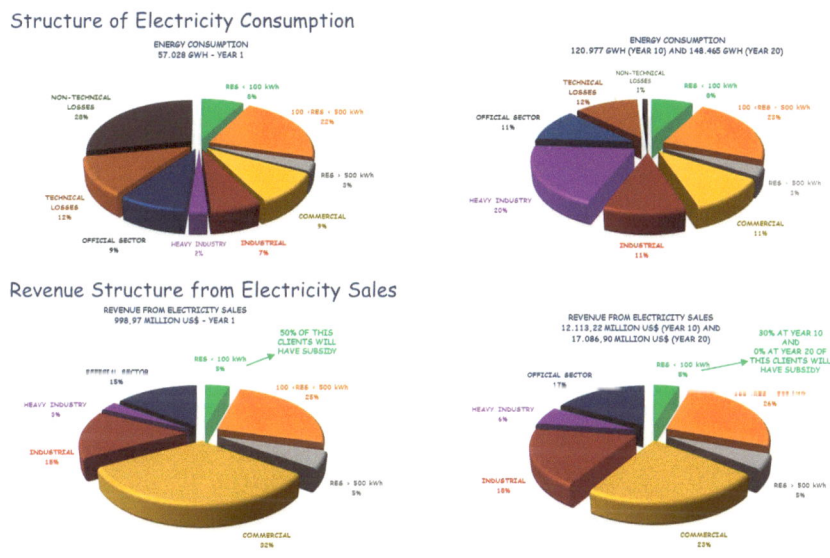

The average growth rate of income obtained for the first decade is 32%, due to the initial adjustment that must be made in the rates of each consumption sector. For the second decade, income maintains the same projected average growth rate of energy consumption, which is 3.5%, as shown in CHART 18.

CHART 18
INCOME PROJECTION FROM ELECTRICITY SALES (US$)

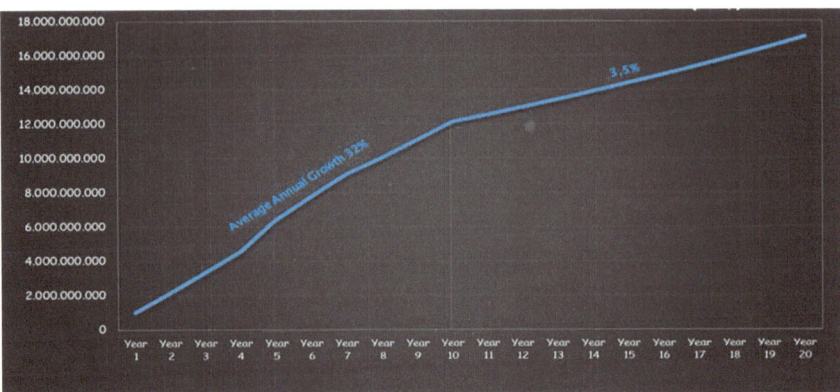

We also estimate the capital disbursements to be invested during the first two years, following the quarterly scheme below:

1Q - 15.41%   2Q - 17.33%   3Q - 18.06%   4Q - 15.97%

5Q - 11.11%   6Q - 9.79%   7Q - 7.23%   8Q - 5.10%

CHART 19 shows the Capital Disbursement Schedule required to recover the SEN (16,500 MMUS$). This capital outlay must occur during the first two years. This is based on the action program: 90 Days, 90 Weeks, 10 Years, and 20 Years, thoroughly described and supported with our engineering and economic arguments.

CHART 19
CAPITAL DISBURSEMENTS (US$)

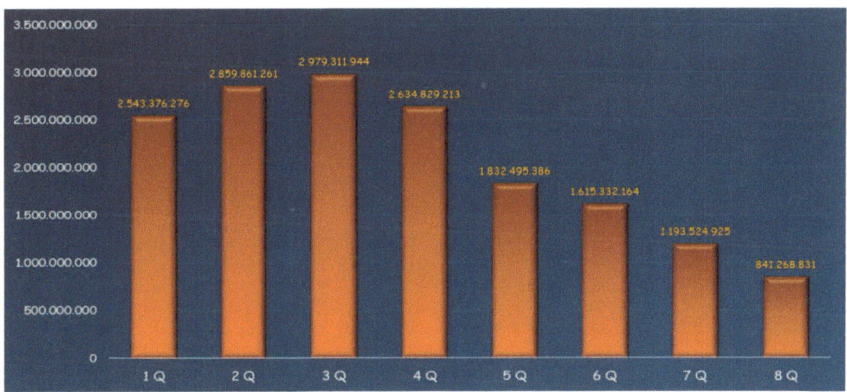

Subsequently, with the application of the set of basic premises for the financing model, the result is shown in CHART 20. The interest payment for the first ten years will amount to 20,264.48 million USD, representing 30.05% of income from electricity sales.

In the second decade, capital and interest payments will amount to 30,892.54 million USD, representing 21.00% of income from electricity sales.

CHART 20
RESULTS OF THE 16,500 MM US$ FINANCING MODEL.
INCOME AND EXPENSES

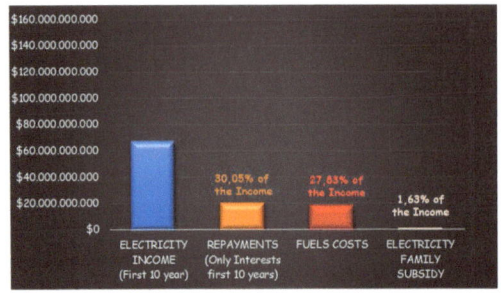

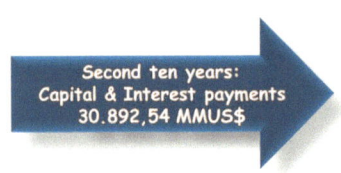
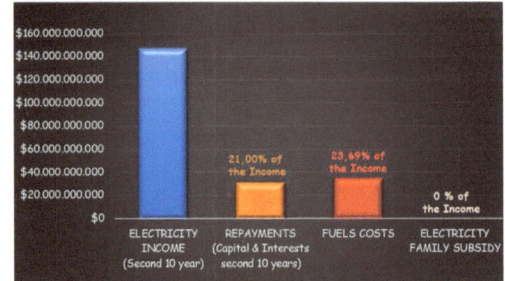

The following CHART 21 illustrates the financing model in two parts.

The image above, highlighted with a blue square, shows the interest payment during the first ten years, amounting to 20,264.48 MMUSD. This payment is offset by two sources of income: electricity sales (represented by the mustard-colored bar) from the electricity sector and fuel sales (represented by the red-colored bar).

The image below shows the scenario for the second ten years, where the combined payment of interest and capital amounts to 30,892.54 MMUSD. This period achieves higher income compared to the first decade, resulting in a positive balance.

CHART 21
FINANCING MODEL USING AN ELECTRICITY TAX ON THE BARREL OF OIL PRODUCED BY PDVSA

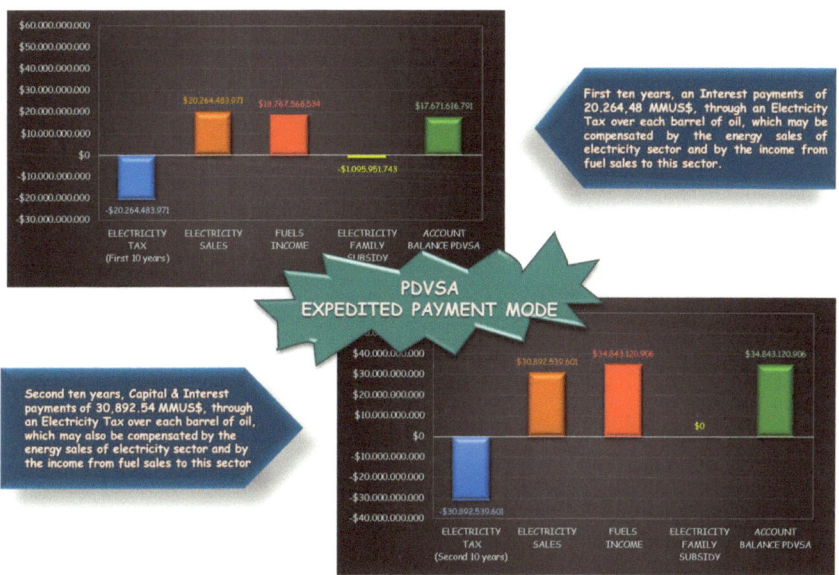

The financing model shown in CHART 21 above is based on the premise of establishing a tax on electricity for each barrel of oil produced and using PDVSA as an expedited means of payment.

CHARTS 20 and 21 detail the payment of interest on the financing of 20,264.48 MMUSD, through the aforementioned tax on each barrel of oil produced. This tax is offset by the income associated with the sales of electricity and fuel to the electrical sector. Thus, the balance of the PDVSA account, as a means of expedited payment for the first 10 years of financing, reaches 17,671,616,791.00 USD.

During the second 10 years, the principal payment plus interest reaches 30,892,539,601.00 USD. With the compensation associated with the income from the sales of electricity and fuel, the balance for PDVSA at the end of the financing period will be 34,843,120,906.00 USD.

CHART 22 summarizes the loan repayments over the period of 20 years.

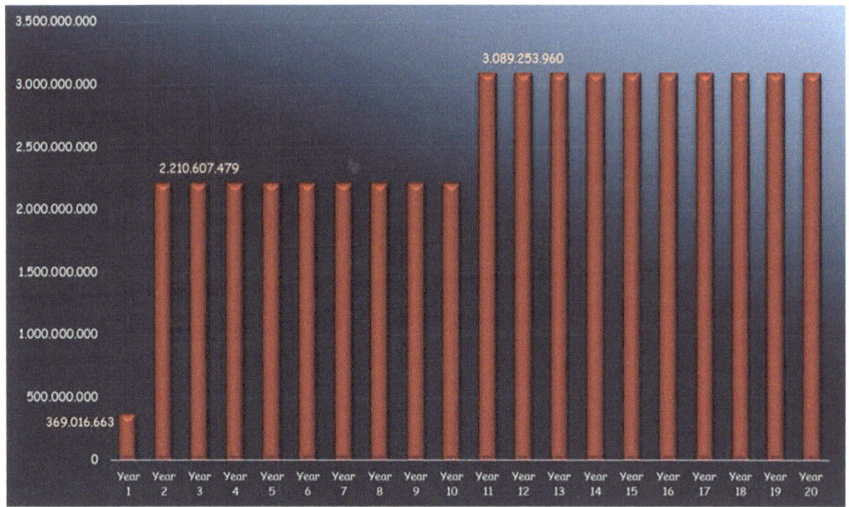

CHART 22
REPAYMENTS (US$)

Finally, maintaining the systemic thinking model with which we have addressed the problem at hand and its respective solution, CHART 23 shows the review we carried out to verify the sustainability of the Project. We prioritized four factors, of which the ECONOMIC was already commented on.

Secondly, the TECHNICAL feasibility is guaranteed by the existence in Venezuela of machinery, experienced personnel, and equipment at disposal.

Thirdly, we analyzed the SOCIAL factor, where family subsidies and Restorative Circles were calibrated. These units pursue communication and mutual understanding of responsibilities and needs of the parties involved, with the aim of guaranteeing social harmony and governance. In this regard, we included 15 million USD to finance the programs that arise from this alliance.

Fourth, but not least, the INSTITUTIONAL impact was considered, which improves the quality of life, strengthens and activates public and private institutions, attracts foreign and national investment, expands energy security, and improves the image of the country internally and externally.

CHART 23
SUSTAINABILITY OF THE PLAN

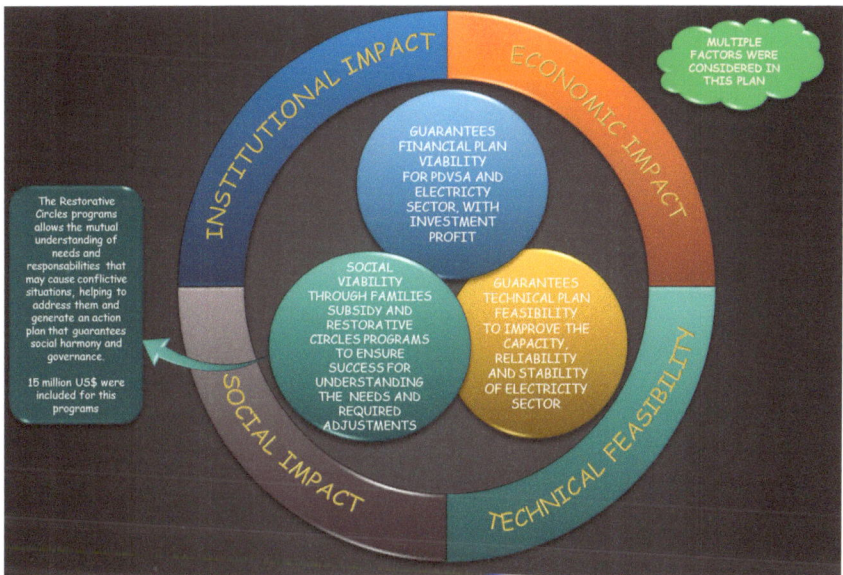

CLARIFICATION

The proposed financing model takes into account the possibility that financiers can belong to the private international sector. In this sense, an open capital company will be created, led by the financial institution that provides the funds. The Venezuelan state will appear as the owner of the Transmission System, which will have to be transferred to the aforementioned company for its commercial value at the time of the transaction. Consequently, it will have a minority stake.

I cannot fail to mention the memorable phrase that John F. Kennedy said in his first speech before the US Congress on the occasion of being named president (20/01/61):

"Don't think what your country can do for you. Think what you can do for your country" (14).

We must internalize the idea of launching our **future financial developments completely open to foreign or national private investment, with free competition,** both in the electricity sector and in all activities of the future reconstruction of our dear and beloved homeland, VENEZUELA. That course of action will give us unique credibility.

To say goodbye, I want to share with the reader some of my feelings. It is important that you know that I understand the seriousness of the situation our country is experiencing. I won't try to downplay it. However, I wish to leave you with the wise words of the poet Rabindranath Tagore for reflection: "If you cry because you can't see the sun, your tears won't let you see the stars" (15)

… And I, together with you, want to see the stars.

Your friend,
Blas Herrera Pérez

(1) Peter Checkland, Metodología de Sistemas Blandos (2004)

(2) Neufville y Keeney en https://www.sciencedirect.com/science/article/pii/0041164773900063

(3-7) https: //Bancomundial.org

(4) https://www.imf.org/es/About/Factsheets/IMF-Lending

(5) https://www.france24.com/ es/20180909-islandia-10-anos-despues-de-la-crisis

(6) https:// es Wikipedia.org/crisis_ financiera _en _ Irlanda

(7) https://www.bcie.org/paises-socios/fundadores/el-salvador

(8) https://elpais.com/america/termometro-social/2023-07-26/hidrogeno-verde-clave-para-la- transicion-energetica-en-chile.html.

(9) Extracted from "Figuraciones mías", Fernando Savater, 2013

(10) British Petroleum BP.org

(11-12) Sysware. Sistemas estables. J.M. García, 2004.

(13) (7) https://www.bcie.org/paises-socios/fundadores/el-salvador

(14) Joan Carles Mélich, La fragilidad de mundo: Ensayo sobre un tiempo precario, 2021.

(15) Rabindranath Tagore | Biography, Poems, Short histories.

www.ingramcontent.com/pod-product-compliance
Lightning Source LLC
LaVergne TN
LVHW070046070526
838200LV00028B/406